TO STAR THE DARK

First published in 2021 by
The Dedalus Press
13 Moyclare Road
Baldoyle
Dublin D13 K1C2
Ireland

www.**dedaluspress**.com

Copyright © Doireann Ní Ghríofa, 2021

ISBN 978-1-910251-86-7 (paperback)
ISBN 978-1-910251-87-4 (hardback)

All rights reserved.
No part of this publication may be reproduced in any form
or by any means without the prior permission
of the publisher.

The moral rights of the author have been asserted.

Dedalus Press titles are available in Ireland
from Argosy Books (www.argosybooks.ie) and in the UK
from Inpress Books (www.inpressbooks.co.uk).

Cover image by Tom Climent, with thanks.
See also *www.tomcliment.com*.

The Dedalus Press receives financial assistance from
The Arts Council / An Chomhairle Ealaíon.

TO STAR THE DARK

DOIREANN NÍ GHRÍOFA

DEDALUS PRESS

ACKNOWLEDGEMENTS

Heartfelt thanks to all who supported me during the years that these poems were composed: The Lannan Foundation, The Arts Council of Ireland, the Rooney Family, the Seamus Heaney Centre for Poetry, the Midsummer Festival, and Éigse Michael Hartnett. *Buíochas ó chroí libh go léir*. I'm grateful to the teachers who care for my children as I work, and to Rose and Marian whose kindness let me write when my children were little. My thanks, also, to the editors who published early versions of these poems in *Fallow, Image Magazine, New Hibernia Review, Poetry Magazine, Poetry Ireland Review, Poetry Review, Port, Salamander, The Irish Review, The Irish Times, The Stinging Fly, Women and the Irish Revolution,* and *Winter Papers*. 'Another Orgasm Against a Wall' and 'Escape: A Chorus in Capes' were commissioned for the book *Nine Silences*, a collaboration with artist Alice Maher (Salvage Press, 2018). 'Lunulae' was commissioned by Tadhg O'Sullivan for his film 'To the Moon.' My gratitude to those who lent their thoughts to these poems: Pat Boran, Seán Hewitt, Cal Doyle and James Harpur. All my love to my children, as always, and to Tim, for everything.

Contents

A Spell in a Shed / 9
While Bleeding / 10
Dancing in the Demesne / 12
Brightening / 13
A Spell in a Ruin / 15
Prayer / 16
A Fragment Torn from the Book of Showers / 17
How the Crocus Climbs, How the Roses Rise / 18
Bloom / 20
A Snippet 5.6 Seconds Long
of a Subterranean Waterfall / 21
Under the City, A Light in a Cave / 22
Triolet in an Inherited Plastic Laundry Basket / 23
Hearing The Boatman's Call
in a Boston Laundromat / 24
A Nocturne Spun of Lust and Lunar Dust / 26
Between Nectarines / 27
Seven Postcards from a Hospital / 29
Hive Lullaby / 36
False Friends / 37
A Jaw, Ajar / 38
An Experiment to Engineer
an Inheritance of Fear / 40
Two Daydreams / 42
At Derrynane, I Think of Eibhlín Dubh Again / 44
A Spell in Sunshine / 45
Maude, Enthralled / 46
When Night Draws its Breath / 50

Escape: A Chorus in Capes / 51
Waking Again / 52
Lunulae / 53
Craquelure / 54
In Albumen, In Pixels, In Bricks / 56
Another Orgasm Against a Wall / 58
Charm and a Cage / 61
At Half Eleven in the Mutton Lane Inn,
I am Fire, Slaughter, Dead Starlings / 63
A Letter to the Stranger
Who Will Dissect My Brain / 65

NOTES / 69

*The past has come apart
events are vagueing*
— Mina Loy

*Has the day invaded the night,
or has the night invaded the day?*
— Louise Bourgeois

To You.
Thank you for lifting these poems to the light.

A Spell in a Shed

Lambkin, sheepskin,
blood, shanks, mutton,

pocketfuls of black wool
when shears sing of cutting.

Darken, quicken,
mud and mother;

the blade grows dull,
the shepherdess sullen.

While Bleeding

In a vintage boutique on Sullivan's Quay,
I lift a winter coat
with narrow bodice, neat lapels,
tight waist, a fallen hem.

It's far too expensive for me,
but the handwritten label [1915]
brings it to my chest in armfuls of red.

In that year, someone drew a blade
through a bolt of fabric and stitched this coat
into being. I carry it

to the dressing room, slip
my arms in; silk lining spills
against my skin. To clasp
the belt is to draw a slow breath
as a cramp curls again
where blood stirs and melts.

In glass, I am wrapped in old red –
    red pinched into girl cheeks
    and smeared from torn knees,
    lipstick blotted in tissue, scarlet
    concealed in pale sheets, all the red
    that fell into pads and rags –
    the weight of red, the wait for red
    that we share.
    In the mirror, the coat blushes.

This pocket may once have sheltered
something precious: a necklace, a love letter,
or a fresh egg, feather-warm, held gently
so it couldn't crack, couldn't leak through seams,
so it couldn't stain the dress within.

Dancing in the Demesne

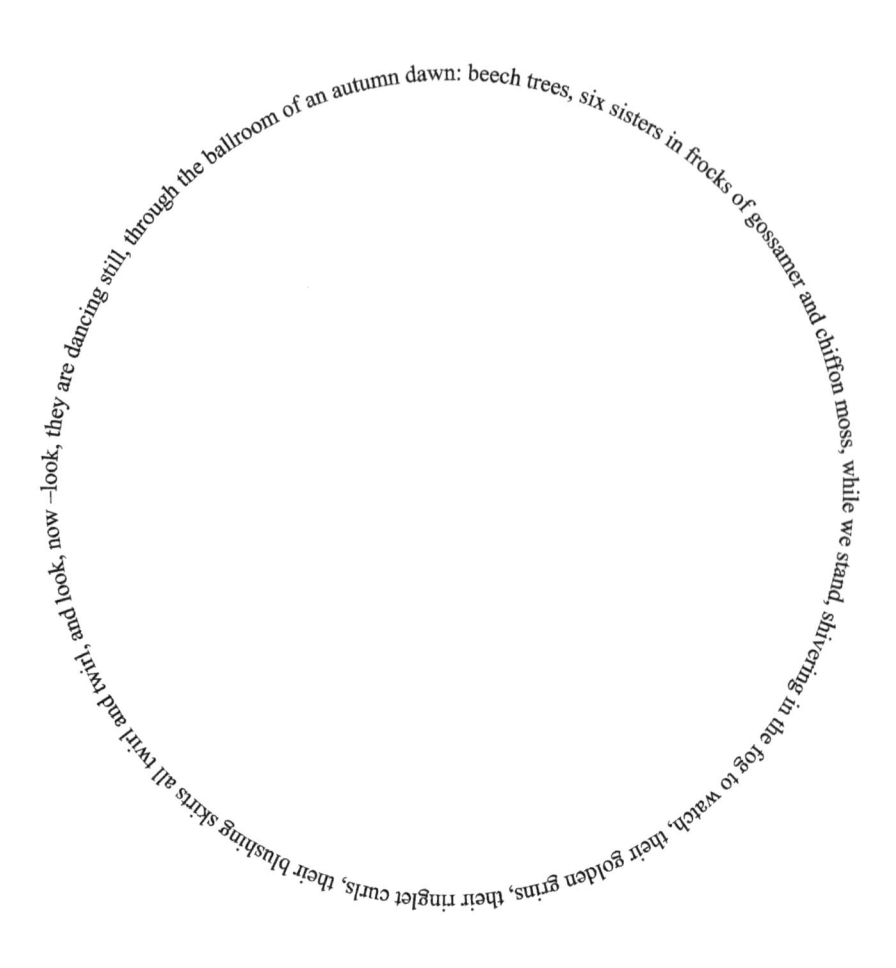

through the ballroom of an autumn dawn: beech trees, six sisters in frocks of gossamer and chiffon moss, while we stand, shivering in the fog to watch, their golden grins, their ringlet curls, their blushing skirts all twirl and twirl, and look, now –look, they are dancing still,

Brightening

'and the fire brought a crowd in'
— Austin Clarke

When night stirs in me,
it brings no dream of sea, no quench,
no liquid reprieve. Night raises only
the old roar, sets the stench of petrol spilling once more.

O Night. How polite, the strangers who pushed me
to choose heirlooms to send out to safety.
How their smiles grew shaky when I chose
only the front door key. O Home.

Down in the night-damp grass, I stood alone.
Men watched me from the lawn;
I knew their mute gaze – grown grey, grown cold –
as I knew all the women huddled on the gravel,
how they folded whispers in their shawls.

I turned from them and watched it begin.
The Brightening. Our windows, lit. One
by one from within. Cellar to hall to kitchen.
How the ballroom shone. How the library blazed.

If brigade bells sang, they sang in vain, for flames
were already spilling up the drapes, to erase
every hand and face from their gilt frames,
swiping china and ivory knives, fox-furs and silks,
tugging precious stones from each brooch's golden grip.

Ghosts, those flames, racing up the stairs,
sending smoke through slates,
a vast constellation of sparks to star the dark.
O paraffin splash. O ash.

When the eaves creaked, one boy came to me,
shy grin turned jeer:
The house of the thief is known by the trees.
To leave was to feel my back gleam.

Now, I may have no home of my own,
I may be alone, but I am not meek. No.
I am a stone released from old gold,
and O, I blaze a Sunday through every week.

A Spell in a Ruin

Hoofprint, lichen, slugs on rubble:
all that's left of the old rooms, crumpled.

Ruin. Ruin: the lintels stumble.
Glint, lost teaspoons. Blow, gold curtains.

Prayer

In my childhood bedroom, the wind is shivering
the curtains, beckoning darkness in again.
Every night of my girl-years

I knelt here,
lips trembling with inherited words
and inherited fears.

Those whisperings
made such clenched visions spin
– red fissures, thorns, weeping women –

while I knelt and begged my small desires
from the dark that fired
behind my eyelids.

Tonight,
you tiptoed to my door,
while everyone else slept,
to sit on my bed, naked.

Lamplit,
you grow a yellow halo,
and again, I kneel
in the dark

below.
From my lips,
the old words leap:
Oh god, oh god, oh please.

A Fragment Torn from the Book of Showers

So throw open
the drapes

and praise
the rain,

how swiftly
it slips us

through
the double

words
it gives us.

Open your mouth,
pronounce

the *fall*
in asphalt,

the *is*
in drizzle,

the *awe*
in squall.

How the Crocus Climbs, How the Roses Rise

> *Il pleure dans mon cœur*
> *comme il pleut sur la ville.*
> — Paul Verlaine

In the Jardin du Luxembourg, we touch lips
to the lids of takeaway cafés au lait
and raspberry pastries. We don't speak.

Akhmatova and Modigliani sat here too,
laughing in the rain, while at their feet,
drenched petals bloomed.

Now the crocuses are opening again,
all yellows and blues. Love,
I've kept a secret from you.

This morning, I snuck from our room,
hurried here and dug,
my hands fast in the dirt,

and into that hollow I sank
a bulb, whispering your name
as I pressed the soil snug.

Every spring, the earth here
will break and bloom, a single stem
hefting a crown of blue.

On another afternoon, Anna
stood outside Amedeo's studio
with armfuls of red. No voice

answered hers; closed roses flew
from her fingers instead. Maybe
she smiled as she threw those stems

through his window again and again.
Maybe she knew what they would do
in the shadows of that locked room.

Bloom

They bloom in old books,
from stems plucked on warm afternoons,
pressed here to flatten, then forgotten.

The clock stops.
The garden is lost. Into the fog
go the children.

Still, the drab spines. Still,
the squashed blossoms
in their meadows of type,

where four buttercups lie
by a stowaway daisy
with old yellow eyes.

A Snippet 5.6 Seconds Long of a Subterranean Waterfall

So fast, this child learns to scroll
and swipe. When he finds my phone
he hides, sliding past his own old eyes

until he reaches his favourite clip:
Ailwee again, there it is. The cave,
the cave, the same old darkness,

the waterfall lit by a dozen flashes,
which he watches, as we did, transfixed.
Every time he touches it, it spills again

to his fingertip, obedient and quick.
Again, he presses ▶, and again the dark wakes,
filling the screen with falling amber flames.

He stares, and we stare at his face,
how it reflects that past, even as it turns away:
luminous, luminous and suddenly strange.

Under the City, A Light in a Cave

The lift falls fast
to the cellar carpark,

its dim walls scrawled
and pockmarked.

No candle
blinks here,

but a screen
bears the prayer

programmed to repeat
in all coin machines.

Change is possible.
It gleams.

Triolet in an Inherited Plastic Laundry Basket

See these seasons of sway,
and your days, ah, your days, all carried away
in the armfuls of laundry you wash, peg, fold away,
oh see these seasons of sway …
but the garments you fold aren't yours, are they?
And when you scold, it's your own child-voice echoing "OK, OK."
See? These seasons do sway,
and your days are a daze, all carried away.

Hearing *The Boatman's Call* in a Boston Laundromat

When I was 22, my day off was Tuesday,
and, come midday, I'd be ding-dinging through
the same grimy door on Massachusetts Avenue,

my hair piled high and loose, soft
jeans frayed, earlobes silver-hooped.
I was always dazed, thirsty, slightly stoned,

hip-hefting the same old basket
filled with the same old clothes.
I never had enough change, no,

I always had to feed another dollar to the coin machine,
before scooping dropped quarters up from the floor,
and spill-spooning detergent into the drawer.

Through that thin window, it all churned,
wet and muddled, but sometimes, I'd glimpse
a garment becoming itself, if only for a moment –

the collar of a work-shirt's blue glance back,
or a jeans pocket kissing its cheek
against the glass. Next, they spiralled

damp to dry, all fly and fall and fall and fly,
while beyond the spool of walkman songs,
beyond *(Are You) The One That I've Been Waiting For?*

and *Where Do We Go Now But Nowhere*,
all I could see was washing machines,
as though many clock-faces had sprung open

to give a glimpse of cogs and springs,
all spinning, all whirring in foamy momentum,
every Tuesday afternoon, when I lived in the distance.

A Nocturne Spun of Lust and Lunar Dust

if it's true
that the moon knows no wind
to un-spin the footprints of men, then
they must be there still, those marks
made by human touch,
chilled in clumps of lunar dust,

invisible to us,
though we don't see much
beyond burst buttons and undone skirts,
where curtains spill open to moonlit skin
and your lips cling to my clavicle
as though they always will.

Between Nectarines

All winter, the infant
inside me dreams
of nectarines,

she thirsts
for their dimpled clefts, blushing
skins, sweet torn flesh.

With each urge,
I think of my grandmother's
mother, a stranger, girl

who crossed an ocean
to scour bedpans
and polish brass,

who returned, rapt
in old red skirts
and a new cloche hat,

dreaming all her lost fruits
back. Not our crab-apples
or blackberries, no,

she spoke of blueberries
and nectarines,
of mangos.

I stand between them
when my teeth touch the husk –
hardy cargo

clenched between
future and past – and within,
a small seed. All winter, she dreams.

Seven Postcards from a Hospital

i.

The afternoon that I walk through hospital doors, I walk away from a poem in which I've grown a forest. Left: the laptop cursor, blinking in my absence until the screen darkens. From the machine to which I'm fastened, a long scroll unravels. Night falls in the forest.

ii.

Fourteen people in blue gowns and masks are working in my body, while I lie on a table, naked from the breast down. A dream of spinal morphine rewrites me, until I see – I see my daughter, and then she's away in a blanket. Beyond the glass a sapling appears to nod at me.

iii.

Minus One: the baby is hurried to Intensive Care. I weep on floor three, tethered by drip, cannula and catheter. I resent my deadened legs; I fret that she may be waking alone, blinking in my absence.

iv.

When I descend to the basement, I find her in an incubator, sleeping on her belly, my Persephone. A bruise holds her hand where blood was drawn to be sent abroad. The word I hear most now is blood — *Blood blood* — *Blood blood* — a steady thud that reverberates in my head like a pulse. Diagrams learned for long-ago exams return to me: the arterial tree, branching, branching: sturdy heart to minuscule capillary.

v.

Here is Neonatal ICU. Here, a plastic chair. Here, my seeping, unseen wound. Here, my baby, and here, my ache. Today, she will not feed. She will not wake. Every hour, I scrub my arms with red surgical soap from fingertip to elbow. I sit by her incubator and cry. My hands turn scales. My eyes: red, then dry. I cry. I laugh. I cry.

vi.

The baby lies very still among tubes and wires. New nurses always smile when they say we look alike. I doubt them, but the mirror sees the resemblance: I, too, am dark-haired, pale and trembling.

vii.

When she opens her eyes, I think of Francis Bacon's studio with its forests of brushes and tins, easels and slashed canvases, his walls daubed in vivid blotches, and, beyond it all, one large mirror. Circular. Her eye, when it opens, is dark as a mirror at night. Her eye, when it opens, seeks me out like a mouth.

Hive Lullaby

Unkempt, nectar-flecked, I lurch
from the pulse of breast pumps
– all rush and suck and rush and suck –
to reach your brood chamber, little one.

Of all the voices you'll hear,
mine will be first. So I say
froth and *cusp*, say *rushed*
and *blood*, I tremble and say
cloud and *dandelion* and *plum*.

All night, I murmur the gold dust
that will hold us. I say *foxglove,
hum, bumble, tortoise* – oh love,
I'll learn the verse if you sing the chorus.

False Friends

The Irish for history is star.
The Irish for teach is moon.
The Irish for light is loss.
The Irish for secret is ruin.

Perhaps this is why
night skies catch our eye,
luring us to learn
by what light still shines.

A Jaw, Ajar

> *Cé cheangail ceangal eadrainn,*
> *A theanga seo leath-liom?*
> — Seán Ó Ríordáin

> cur i gcéill: *a pretence, masquerade, a sham*

Suppose
you hold a jawbone
so old that its chin has split.

Suppose the professor explains: *derelict*
workhouse – Famine-era – a mass grave.
In his fist, a broken grin.

He says, *generous*
selection of fragments, says *incremental*
dentine collagen analysis.

For him, you must say when starvation set in.
So hold the bone: two neat halves, one in each hand.
Bring them together and see it: full, skinned,

a stubbled chin, a cheek once patted,
kissed, hit, a mouth that knew
the speech and spit of one warm tongue.

Lift it to your ear; try to lure a voice
from elsewhere, spoken or sung.
You wish you could return to it

a word that once echoed
through its hollows,
but your voice catches in your throat.

Suppose the professor smiles:
A fine specimen, this mandible.
What would you call it in Gaelic?

You stutter, trying to say *corrán géill*,
but your split tongue fails, and the only
sound you make is *cur i gcéill*.

An Experiment to Engineer an Inheritance of Fear

HYPOTHESIS:

This study will quantify how descendants shudder in response to the memories of another.

PHASE 1:

Every time subjects are exposed to electric stimuli, the target smell will be released.

> *Call it shock.*
> *Tie it to the smell of rot.*
>
> *Give her terror in a meadow.*
> *Bind her fear to a black potato.*

PHASE 2:

Shielded from fear and hunger, subsequent generations will appear well-adjusted.

PHASE 3:

When exposed to the ancestral scent, great-grandchildren will show signs of distress.

What might she conclude from this?

Old scars sing, even in absence.

Two Daydreams

In an exam hall, a girl of fifteen sighs,
then writes:
>   *By 1850, a million were dead
>   and a million had fled.*

The pencil pauses. She gnaws a nail,
while far away another girl wakes.

Daydreamt: her mother, calling her
for a *luathóg* baked in embers,
and she can almost taste it,
dipped in egg and turned in butter,
can almost hear a hen chuckle,
or the gurgle of her baby brother,

but home dies with her opening eyes,
as dark dies in daylight, and in dying,
it conjures her hands, still alive,
the lunulae dark where she tried
and failed to put the last face away.
Too weak to weep, she tugs

a rough blanket over her head,
and tries to go into dream again.
A dash draws her back – perhaps
another mouse too fast to catch –
but again, that sound, until her fingers
fumble out, and there, in the straw by her leg,

is one small egg. Tears, then, as a cluster
of silver cells flicker within, tiny particles
that will bring her daughters and granddaughters
from this egg in her fist. One by one, we
will all come, until another girl of fifteen
sits in the distance, lost in a daydream.

At Derrynane, I Think of Eibhlín Dubh Again

In April – when bog myrtle
flickers through thickets

and crimson stems begin to think
in catkins again,

stretching to a length
that might tickle a girl's knees,

a girl who laughs
as she hurries through trees –

I'm reading your words
Mo chara is m' uan tú,

and wondering again
where they buried you.

If I could find your gravestone,
I'd bring no rose, Eibhlín,

only a fistful of myrtle stems
tied in twine, tugged tight

and neat, to be placed,
gently, at your feet.

A Spell in Sunshine

Come spring, every new leaf
is a silk handkerchief, unfurling
itself, both new and antique,
already lifting cheery farewells,
so green, and so brief.

Maude, Enthralled

for Maude Delap

(i) MORNING

Seventh of ten, little Maude is running
on Valentia Strand again. In her braids,
sea wind unspins, until she skids. Sudden
in the sand, spiked with ink, tentacles spill
from a fleshy pink, and oh!, it stings.

(ii) AFTERNOON

The ocean, alone.　　Alone, the ocean.
And Maude, afloat.　　　Under her boat,
a world　　　　　of hover
and float,　　　of swim and flit
and gilled throats.　　　Maude peers
past ling　　　and dogfish,
past pollock　　　and conger eel,
until she sees　　the tentacles
that she seeks.　　All swell
and release,　　those skewed
globules,　　　crimson- and
blue-streaked.　　Maude considers
how each bell　　draws up handfuls
of itself,　　then lets go.
Maude learns　　　this lesson well;
Maude takes　　notes.

(iii) EVENING

Her hours of dredging, fizzing air into aquaria
and feeding the jellyfish fill her shelves
with specimens, an exhibition of spin and dip.
These clotted blooms cannot hurt her
as words do:
> *No daughter of mine will leave*
> *home, except as a married woman.*

Maude knows the etymology of *captivate*,
how it holds both charm and a cage.

(iv) NIGHT

After nightfall, the jellyfish gnaw at Maude,
they call and call, until at last, she rises,
rubbing her eyelids, with a candlestick in her fist,
its flame sheltered by arthritic fingertips.

To the lab, where her face is mirrored
in bell jars: Maude; Maude; Maude again.
And are they there, still, her specimens?
Or have they perished too?

Only Night tells the truth. Moonlight spells
the evidence in cobwebs, crushed glass and filth.
All the jellyfish, all the liquid once held
in her vessels – long evaporated to silt.

Captive, still, Maude ghosts the dark,
lifting a hand to the imagined glass that always
held her back from the dance. See her, awed
– Maude, our Maude – barefoot, enthralled.

When Night Draws its Breath

Beyond our curtains,
the water's dark silks
sing the old lullaby
of sink and silt,
all laps and slips
and laps and slips,

    until,

        until,

Escape: A Chorus in Capes

we are leaving our babies
fed and warm in their cots

we are leaving dark kitchens
untying apron knots

we are stumbling in nightdresses
through doors left unlocked

we are grasping towards water
past badger and fox

no moon, no, no star
when we wrench off our socks

only darkness so sharp
it fills pockets with rocks

we walk into rivers   we walk into seas
we walk into lakes   we will never speak

we are swallowed by water
we never will rise

we return through dark borders
leaving old lives behind

Waking Again

for Savita Halappanavar

When I close my eyes, she's opening hers
to find the procedure complete and the hospital asleep.

Her hand lies limp on warm skin –
empty without and empty within.

To hear a small cry is to think
not mine. Still, beyond the sheet,

the faint retreat of footsteps,
and still, her heart beats.

Lunulae

Though it grew dark and darker,
how could we despair

when we remembered the crescents,
pale in each fingernail?

Ten little moons
to glimmer our grip,

slips of brightness that persist,
holding our hands, even in darkness.

Craquelure

Her tracksuit is pink velour,
her earlobes prettily golden-hooped,
and she shivers – as we all do –
in this bus queue.

At 5.56, some glitch, some distraction,
some finger twitch slips the phone
from her grip and sends it smashing
into the pavement. We all flinch.

Soon, the bus moves us through streets
and suburbs and into the dark. Night
makes a mirror of the window
and makes me a spy. Sitting behind,

I watch her fingers move fast
on that fractured glass, where digits
progress, still, over her child's smile,
his eyes grown suddenly lined.

A little ink leaks from those rifts,
and it grows dark, oh, it grows dark
and darker. Take us back, driver.
Lurch this bus into reverse.

As a conservator rewinds
a painting's eyes, bring us back.
Let her lift her phone
from the path, intact.

Let her shiver, check the time,
sigh at her child's smile, then
slide the phone back in her pocket,
its digits slipping to 5.59.

In Albumen, In Pixels, In Bricks

I

In pregnancy, a woman carries
a baby's ovaries like little fists

on fallopian wrists.
Through each handful, oocytes wink;

in this, a mother is the eggshell
that lifts her descendants.

II

Two weeks before Christmas,
I'm holding a string of tinsel
when the phone rings.

The landlord wants our home for his son.
I drop the tinsel.
He gives us a month.

On supermarket shelves,
my hand drifts the cardboard shells.
Within, I know, are chalazae threads,

thin filaments that connect each egg's
membrane to its yellow orb. Tender,
translucent, those gentle cords.

III

I scroll and scroll,
but every rent is too expensive for me.
Eventually, I look back instead,
clicking until I am stilled by *'Family at Glenbeigh, 1888'*

with its splintered cabin, the man, the woman,
their barefoot children. I peer at the girl's hands,
but can't quite see what she has, a fistful
of her apron, perhaps, a clutch of wool, or flax.

Her hand exists only in pixels now, this girl
who arrives by optic nerve to live a while
in my mind. I see, then, what she holds. I know
its chalazae grip; I know the gold that floats.

Another Orgasm Against a Wall

Hold my throat and I will sing
to belt buckle click, to fingers and spit,
to skin and brick,

and though it is too dark to see,
I feel each breath move
inside the wall, away from me.

Each sigh of mine turns
firm in there, beyond layers
of plaster and horsehair;

each gasp turns
gold, wedged tight
between old stones.

In Fermoy, an English boy
met a bullet in the street.
His last breath bled into gravel,

setting his brother soldiers roaring up
from the garrison, smashing every merchant's glass,
swearing over armfuls of wares.

Each object floated for one thrown moment,
then slipped through the river's skin –
stockings, wedding rings, cufflinks, all swept away –

all except the clockmaker's display.
His soft velvet tray spent a second
held between belly and bridge,

where the sun's rays lit each pocket-chain
and case, warming every patient face.
Sudden, the plunge

into the river's tumbling suck,
to become wedged tight
in stones and dirt. Stuck.

No chime from murk,
no tick in silt; between those stones,
their hours stilled.

A trout's belly pays no heed
to the intricacies of hairsprings
or escapement wheels,

the river's silver flow cannot
know the convolutions of anchor
or arbour, bezel or bow,

and no one turning from the pub
towards home would check the hour
in the Blackwater's tremble-throat. No.

No one remembered them, not their hands,
not their faces, not the slender apertures
that once moved to the phases of the moon.

I do. I think of them
when my breast is pressed
against a wall again.

I, too, sing nocturnes
of moon and skin,
and in that hymn,

my breath spills
gold between old stones
again. Again.

Charm and a Cage

for Friedrich Gustav Maximilian Schreck

Here, our gaze cannot break
because here, my screen binds our stares.

In this GIF, you exist, Friedrich, you do;
I click it to resurrect you, bringing you back

as Nosferatu – your grip firm on a splintered pane,
your nails clipped into cartoon blades.

In Slovakia, I know, it grew cold,
the day they filmed your castle stare. You wandered

away and found a forest there, where you lost yourself
in thornberries, in birdsong and sweet, cold air.

Decades later, in interviews, the crew still spoke
of how *peculiar* you seemed, how *weird*, this man,

calm only in the company of trees, but Friedrich,
dear Friedrich, your clenched jaw remembered

the trenches, didn't it?, the screaming horses,
the bloodied bayonets, the stench of corpses.

There, there – now you can rest,
my handsome marionette. Your ghost

is safe, you mustn't fret –
I've saved you

here, in my screen, cherished
captive, peering back at me.

At Half Eleven in the Mutton Lane Inn, I am Fire, Slaughter, Dead Starlings

Though this pub is crammed
with laughter, I feel your stare.
It burns.

If you continue,
I'll tell you of 1622
when a lightning cloud

shadowed this city,
flinging sparks on thatch
that pulsed to flame.

People stumbled over each other
through laneways, clutching children
to their chests, weeping, afraid,

while fire bloomed along the paths
where they ran, and fell,
and ran.

After the fire,
those who survived spoke
of the omen of a fortnight before,

when two murmurations of starlings
clashed in the sky, flinging themselves
at each other, high and wild,

until small corpses thumped into gutters
and ripped wings cobbled the streets,
leaving the paths all bird-bloodied,

all blush and trembling. For hours,
those birds' tiny magnet-hearts jerked
toward each other, as though

they couldn't help themselves
in shiver and grasp and shatter,
their bodies swooning and falling,

falling into each other
– a thousand small deaths –
except, listen,

in those days,
they didn't call them starlings,
they called them stares.

So, you see, I will say, stares spark fires
that cannot be quenched, stares cause
children to weep, clutched tight to chests.

Turn away,
I will say.
Find someone else.

A Letter to the Stranger Who Will Dissect My Brain

For months, you worked
scissors and scalpel

through elbow and knuckle,
ligament and lung.

I felt you gasp, the morning
you folded my face back like a mask.

For you, my head was unsealed
by chisel and skull key, so that today,

you may raise the calvarium
and see my brain there,

cold and grey, under dura mater
and spider-web membrane.

For this moment, dear stranger,
I leave you a gift, a double word –

foscladh – which can both open,
and throw sheet lightning.

Know that when you unlock my brain
with your blade, synaptic flashes

will flare over your own grey landscape.
Your brain will blaze bright,

alive and wild, and I,
I will be the light.

NOTES

Brightening: During the war years of the early 1920s in Ireland, many mansions of the aristocracy were burned.

A Fragment Torn from the Book of Showers is an invention, neither a fragment nor an artefact from any medieval Books of Hours.

How the Crocus Climbs, How the Roses Rise: "When it was drizzling (it very often rains in Paris), Modigliani walked with an enormous and very old black umbrella. We sat sometimes under this umbrella on the bench in the Luxembourg Gardens. There was a warm summer rain; nearby dozed *le vieux palais à l'Italien*, while we in two voices recited from Verlaine, whom we knew well by heart, and we rejoiced that we both remembered the same work of his … One day there was a misunderstanding about our appointment, and when I called for Modigliani, I found him out – but I decided to wait for him for a few minutes. I held an armful of red roses. The window, which was above the locked gates of the studio, was open. To while away the time, I started to throw the flowers into the studio. Modigliani didn't come, and I left. When I met him, he expressed his surprise about my getting into the locked room while he had the key. I explained how it happened. 'It's impossible – they lay so beautifully.'" (from 'Amedeo Modigliani' by Anna Akhmatova, translated by Djemma Bider in *The New York Review of Books* (July 17, 1975).

Under the City, a Light in a Cave: a response from the depths to Niamh Prior's *'Multi-Storey'*.

Hearing The Boatman's Call *in a Boston Laundromat: The Boatman's Call* (1997) is an album by Nick Cave and the Bad Seeds, from which both song titles towards the end of this poem are also drawn.

Seven Postcards from a Hospital: each of these postcards was addressed, in the first case, to my dear friend Sara Baume.

An Experiment to Engineer an Inheritance of Fear: see Dias & Ressler (2014) 'Parental olfactory experience influences behaviour and neural structure in subsequent generations' *Nature Neuroscience*, 17, 89–96.

At Derrynane, I Think of Eibhlín Dubh Again: Eibhlín Dubh Ní Chonaill, author of 'Caoineadh Airt Uí Laoghaire' (1773).

Maude, Enthralled: Maude Delap (1866–1953) was a self-educated authority on marine biology. In 1915, she was at work in Reenelllen House, Valentia Island, studying the life-cycles of jellyfish. The italicised quote – reportedly spoken by Maude's father – is documented in Anne Byrne's essay 'Untangling the Medusa'. I offer my gratitude to Dorothy Cross for introducing me to Delap through her artwork 'Medusae' (2003).

Waking, Again: A recurring dream, this poem is a text that wished to be rewritten, as I wish this event could be rewritten.

Another Orgasm Against a Wall: For an account of this incident as revealed by a local subaquatic diving club, see Timmy Carey's *Subaquatic Memories of Turbulent Times in Fermoy* at blackwatersubaqua.ie

Craquelure: the web of fine cracks that develop on a painting's surface as it ages. It is believed that this word first sprang from French into English usage between 1910 and 1915.

Charm and a Cage: Schreck entered the German army in 1915; he subsequently played the vampire in *Nosferatu, eine Symphonie des Grauens* (1922). A GIF is a brief, soundless, looping clip. The etymology of 'captivate' suggests both enthrallment and (in an obsolete 16th century usage) entrapment.

In Albumen, In Pixels, In Bricks: The albumen print referred to in this poem was created by Francis Guy, 1760–1820, and may be found in the Seán Sexton photography archive.

At Half Eleven in the Mutton Lane Inn, I am Fire, Slaughter, Dead Starlings: for further historical context, see 'Atlas of Cork City' (eds. Crowley, Devoy, Linehan, O'Flanagan, Murphy, 2005).

Lightning Source UK Ltd.
Milton Keynes UK
UKHW042021010221
378072UK00001B/34